Profiles in American History

The Life and Times of

PATRICK HENRY

Mitchell Lane
PUBLISHERS

P.O. Box 196 · Hockessin, Delaware 19707

South Huntington Pub. Lib.
145 Pidgeon Hill Rd.
Huntington Sta., N.Y. 11746

Profiles in American History

Titles in the Series

The Life and Times of

Alexander Hamilton
Benjamin Franklin
Betsy Ross
Eli Whitney
George Rogers Clark
Hernando Cortés
John Adams
John Cabot
John Hancock
John Peter Zenger
Nathan Hale
Patrick Henry
Paul Revere
Samuel Adams
Sir Walter Raleigh
Susan B. Anthony
Thomas Jefferson
William Penn

Profiles in American History

The Life and Times of

PATRICK HENRY

Susan Harkins and
William H. Harkins

Copyright © 2007 by Mitchell Lane Publishers, Inc. All rights reserved. No part of th book may be reproduced without written permission from the publisher. Printed a bound in the United States of America.

Printing   1   2   3   4   5   6   7   8   9

Library of Congress Cataloging-in-Publication Data
Harkins, Susan Sales.
   The life and times of Patrick Henry/by Susan Harkins and William H. Harkins.
     p. cm. — (Profiles in American history)
   Includes bibliographical references and index.
   ISBN 1-58415-438-1 (library bound: alk. paper)
    1. Henry, Patrick, 1736-1799—Juvenile literature. 2. Legislators—United States-Biography—Juvenile literature. 3. United States. Continental Congress—Biography-Juvenile literature. 4. Virginia—Politics and government—1775-1783—Juvenile Literature. 5. United States—Politics and government—1775-1783—Juvenile literatu I. Harkins, William H. II. Title. II. Series.
E302.6.H5H28 2006
973.3'092—dc22

                                                         20050285
ISBN-10: 1-58415-438-1   ISBN-13: 978-1-58415-43

ABOUT THE AUTHORS: Susan and Bill Harkins live in Kentucky, where they en writing together for children. Susan has written many books for adults and ch dren. Bill is a history buff. In addition to writing, Bill is a member of the Kentuc Civil Air Patrol, where he helps Kentuckians prepare for earthquakes and oth natural disasters.

PHOTO CREDITS: Cover, pp. 1, 3: Getty Images; pp. 6, 9, 10: Library of Congre p. 12: Getty Images; p. 15: Corbis; pp. 18, 24, 27, 30: Library of Congress; p. 32: Ge Images; p. 35: Corbis; p. 38: Library of Congress

PUBLISHER'S NOTE: This story is based on the authors' extensive research, wh they believe to be accurate. Documentation of such research is contained on page
    The internet sites referenced herein were active as of the publication date. D to the fleeting nature of some web sites, we cannot guarantee they will all be act when you are reading this book.

                                                                                  P

Profiles in American History

Contents

Chapter One
    The Voice of Revolution 7
    *FYInfo: Patriots Versus Loyalists 11
Chapter Two
    Far From the Watchful Eye of England 13
    FYInfo: Patrick Henry's Views on Slavery 17
Chapter Three
    On His Way 19
    FYInfo: Hanover County Court Days 23
Chapter Four
    A Noble Patriot 25
    FYInfo: Patrick Henry's Resolutions to the Stamp Act 31
Chapter Five
    Forging a Nation 33
    FYI: America's Bill of Rights 42
Chapter Notes 43
Chronology 44
Timeline in History 45
Further Reading 46
    For Young Adults 46
    Works Consulted 46
    On the Internet 46
Glossary 47
Index 48
*For Your Information

On March 23, 1775, Patrick Henry warned the other delegates at the Second Virginia Convention that England was preparing for war, even while it talked of peace. After his inspiring speech, the American colonists finally came to terms with their future—war with England.

CHAPTER 1

The Voice of Revolution

Patrick Henry knew what he faced as he approached St. John's Church on the morning of March 23, 1775. When he walked through the door, he thought about the task before him. He was risking his life for his beliefs: To speak against the king was treason. He must convince the delegates to choose freedom, even at the risk of being hanged.

For months, Henry had heard the sounds of war—not cannon fire, but the angry voices of Patriots and Loyalists. He listened as the colonists argued in their shops, in their churches, and even around their dinner tables. Today's meeting would be no different.

Inside, he greeted the delegates from Virginia who would soon determine the colony's future. Would they remain loyal to the King of England and lose their freedom? Or could he convince them to fight for their freedom and seize independence?

He found St. John's filled to overflowing. People stood in the aisles and sat on windowsills. As he took his place, he saw the set jaws and heard the angry murmurs. First, the Loyalists spoke against the revolution. They knew that Americans and their English cousins would die in a conflict between the colonies and England. They wanted to believe that the colonies could still

CHAPTER 1

reconcile their differences with the king. The Loyalists were persuasive—no one really wanted war.

History might be different if not for Patrick Henry. Patiently, he listened to the Loyalists speak their minds. When Henry finally took the floor, the room fell silent. He was a skillful speaker—one of the best orators of the day. Everyone wanted to hear what he had to say.

Quietly, he thanked the worthy gentlemen who had spoken, but he warned them that he planned to speak his heart and mind.

> Should I keep back my opinions at such a time, through fear of giving offense, I should consider myself as guilty of treason towards my country, and of an act of disloyalty toward the Majesty of Heaven, which I revere above all earthly kings. . . .
>
> I have but one lamp by which my feet are guided, and that is the lamp of experience. I know of no way of judging of the future but by the past. And judging by the past, I wish to know what there has been in the conduct of the British ministry for the last ten years to justify those hopes with which gentlemen have been pleased to solace themselves and the House. Is it that insidious smile with which our petition has been lately received? Trust it not, sir; it will prove a snare to your feet. Suffer not yourselves to be betrayed with a kiss.[1]

Henry was angry not only with the king, who taxed Americans unfairly and sent warships to their harbors. He was also angry with the Loyalists, who trusted the king. Henry knew that while the Loyalists hoped for peace, the king prepared for war.

"Gentlemen may cry, Peace, Peace," he shouted, "but there is no peace. The war is actually begun! The next gale that sweeps from the north will bring to our ears the clash of resounding arms! Our brethren are already in the field! Why stand we here idle?

8

The Voice of Revolution

King George III underestimated the American colonists. He thought he could tax them and control their exploration into the west. Misjudging the independent colonists was a grave error.

What is it that gentlemen wish? What would they have? Is life so dear, or peace so sweet, as to be purchased at the price of chains and slavery?"

Henry bowed his body as if under a heavy burden and clapped his wrists together as if bound by chains.

"Forbid it, Almighty God! I know not what course others may take"—Henry raised his hands above his head, straining against

CHAPTER 1

Beginning April 19, 1775, right after the Battle of Lexington and Concord, the British occupied Boston and lay siege to its busy harbor. The war for independence had begun.

the imaginary chains until they seemed to break and go free; he raised high his right hand, in which he held a letter opener, and cried—"but as for me, give me liberty or give me death!" He plunged the letter opener toward his chest as if he were plunging a dagger into his own heart.[2]

The crowd jumped to their feet. They shouted and cheered for several minutes. Henry's well-chosen words inspired the delegates. With his help, they found the courage to prepare for war against Britain and her king.

Patriots Versus Loyalists

As the flame of revolution swept through the American colonies, the colonists split into three different camps: those who supported a war for independence, those who wanted to remain part of the British empire, and those who didn't care. Each group claimed about a third of the population. The quest for independence wasn't just an American conflict: The concept of American independence also split the English into common camps.

George Washington

Patriots were Americans who wanted to be free of British rule and the tyrannical King George III. They actively prepared for independence—even by force, if necessary. Some Americans called them Whigs after an English political party that wanted the colonies to govern themselves.

On June 15, 1775, Colonel George Washington became the commander in chief of the Continental Army. This regiment was the first official Patriot force, supported by and paid for by the newly formed government, the Continental Congress. The delegates called themselves the Continental Congress because, at the time, the country they were about to liberate didn't exist. The term *continental,* in the absence of a named government, represented the forces well.

Americans who supported King George and Parliament were Loyalists. They believed Americans should remain subject to the king's rule. Some people called them Tories after the British Tory political party. This party thought the king should rule colonies firmly and absolutely. As often as not, Loyalists were simply horrified by the violence a war would wreak on both the Americans and the English. They hoped to avoid war more than they cared about who was in charge.

The colonies weren't the only groups that were divided. Neighbors and even family members disagreed about which side was right in the struggle for independence.

11

Patrick Henry rose from humble beginnings to become one of the greatest American orators. He would learn his dramatic speaking style from emotional preachers he heard as a child.

CHAPTER 2

Far From the Watchful Eye of England

Patrick Henry grew up on Studley Farm, a large plantation in Hanover County, Virginia. His mother, Sarah Winston Syme Henry, inherited the farm from her first husband, John Syme. Sarah was a young wife and mother when she first met John Henry. He lived with the Syme household for a few years after immigrating to the colonies from Scotland in 1727.

When Syme died unexpectedly in 1731, Sarah didn't know what to do. She didn't know how to run the plantation. John Henry was amiable and well educated. He had a small farm next to Sarah's, but he had little money.

After an appropriate mourning period, Sarah Syme and John Henry married. By marrying him, Sarah got a husband and, hopefully, someone who could run her plantation. John Henry got a wife with money, land, and family connections. The match was socially lopsided, but it wasn't unusual for the times.

Despite Sarah's best hopes, John Henry stayed too busy acting as a major in the Virginia militia to manage her property. Often, he drank too much and lost pieces of her property playing cards.

Even so, life was good for young Patrick. Virginia was still an English colony when Patrick was born on May 29, 1736. Like

CHAPTER 2

every other American living in the colonies, Patrick was a subject of the King of England.

Far from England and the king's watchful eye, most Americans grew up with a sense of freedom that few Englishmen or Europeans could understand. Virginia covered most of the present-day states of Virginia, West Virginia, Kentucky, and the southern portions of Ohio, Illinois, and Indiana. There was plenty of room for a young country boy to explore. Land was fertile and the woods were wild. Patrick loved the back country. He spent whole days hunting, fishing, and swimming. He loved to practice birdcalls and just daydream.

Most likely Patrick was somewhat bored in school. He learned his early lessons in a one-room schoolhouse near his home. Then, from the age of ten, he studied with his father after John Henry opened a small school at Studley Farm. From his father he learned Latin, Greek, history, and mathematics. Despite his father's best efforts, Patrick never excelled in any particular subject—except playing in the woods.

Religion was an important part of most every colonist's life, and Patrick's was no exception. John Henry was a member of the Anglican Church, Virginia's established church. Sarah Henry attended Presbyterian services. While young, Patrick often attended services with his mother, but he eventually joined the Anglican Church.

A religious movement known as the Great Awakening swept the colonies when Patrick was a child. Ministers were passionate and used drama to get and keep the congregation's attention. They knew when to shout and when to speak softly. They could easily excite or terrify their audience.

As Sarah and her children rode home from services, she would quiz Patrick about the sermons. Either out of earnest emotion or out of mimicry, Patrick learned to apply the dramatic styles the ministers used. No one knows whether Patrick took the sermons seriously, but certainly his family enjoyed his enthusiasm. He had a reputation for putting on a great show for his mother and siblings.

Far From the Watchful Eye of England

Henry learned his first academic lessons in a one-room schoolhouse. Eventually, he studied with his father. He was an intelligent child, but he preferred playing in the woods to studying.

It's fair to suppose that these preachers influenced Patrick's later speaking style. Patrick was entertaining and apparently talented at swaying folks to his way of thinking, even as a youth. However, it's doubtful that anyone imagined Patrick would eventually be one of history's greatest orators.

When Patrick was fifteen, he left school and home to apprentice as a store clerk. After a year, his father opened a small country store for Patrick and his older brother, William. The store was on the Pamunkey River in the northeastern corner of Hanover County.[1] The river was busy, and John Henry thought the store would get plenty of business. Unfortunately, he hadn't counted on two things—his boys were too generous and too inexperi-

CHAPTER 2

enced. They sold too much on credit. After a year, they had no merchandise and no money to buy new goods. John Henry closed the store and took the boys home.

Returning home a failure at his first business venture was probably hard for Patrick. To make matters worse, he didn't return to his childhood home, Studley Farm. John Syme Jr., Patrick and William's older half brother, inherited Studley Farm while the boys were away. The Henrys moved to Mount Brilliant, a small plantation of several hundred acres.[2]

Patrick didn't seem to stay homesick for long. Soon, he was happy again, courting Sarah Shelton, a pretty girl who lived nearby. In the fall of 1754, Patrick married his beloved Sarah. Both families were against the marriage because Sarah was just sixteen and Patrick, at eighteen, had no means to support a wife and family. The couple got around everyone's objections as "passion had raced ahead of the parson,"[3] and both families quickly agreed to the marriage.

John Shelton, Sarah's father, gave Patrick six slaves and a few hundred acres as Sarah's dowry. The young couple named the farm Piney Slash. Patrick worked hard, but life at Piney Slash was primitive and difficult. Unfortunately for the Henrys, they took up farming in the middle of a drought. Even with six slaves to help, Patrick could barely support his family.

Then tragedy struck. A fire destroyed their small home and almost everything they owned, which wasn't much. Henry sold the slaves and opened another store near Hanover Courthouse.

Unfortunately, he wasn't any smarter about running a business the second time around. He extended too much credit again. The French and Indian War complicated things too. Basically, that war was a French attempt to hold on to its territory in North America. As if the war weren't enough trouble, the weather destroyed the 1758 Virginia tobacco crop.[4] Eventually, Henry closed his second store, heavily in debt.

The situation looked bad for the Henrys, now the parents of two small children. Patrick moved his family into Hanover Tavern, a busy establishment owned by his father-in-law. This decision changed his life—and perhaps the course of history.

Patrick Henry's Views on Slavery

Slaves Working on a Plantation

Like most plantation owners in the colonies, Patrick Henry owned slaves. To his credit, he treated these people relatively well. He made sure they could read, and they learned respectable trades such as leather tanning, carpentry, and blacksmithing. His plantation's success depended on slave labor, and he owned more than ninety slaves when he died. However, all his life he claimed to hate slavery.

"[In] a country, above all others, fond of liberty," he said, "we find Men . . . adopting a Principle as repugnant to humanity as it is inconsistent with the Bible and destructive to Liberty."[5]

Henry believed that eventually Americans would abolish slavery. Until then, he said, "Let us transmit to our descendants together with our Slaves a pity for their unhappy Lot . . . let us treat the unhappy victims with lenity, it is the furthest advance we can make toward justice."[6]

It's difficult to reconcile Henry's feelings about slavery with his actions. His personal objections to slavery and his desire to succeed were in conflict.

"Would anyone believe I am the master of slaves of my own purchase? I am drawn along by the general inconvenience of living here without them. I will not, I cannot justify it."[7]

Henry helped pass laws that put an end to the slave trade from Africa to Virginia and made it easier for owners to free their slaves. By today's standards, we may appreciate Henry's frankness on the subject of slavery, but it is impossible to ignore his hypocrisy.

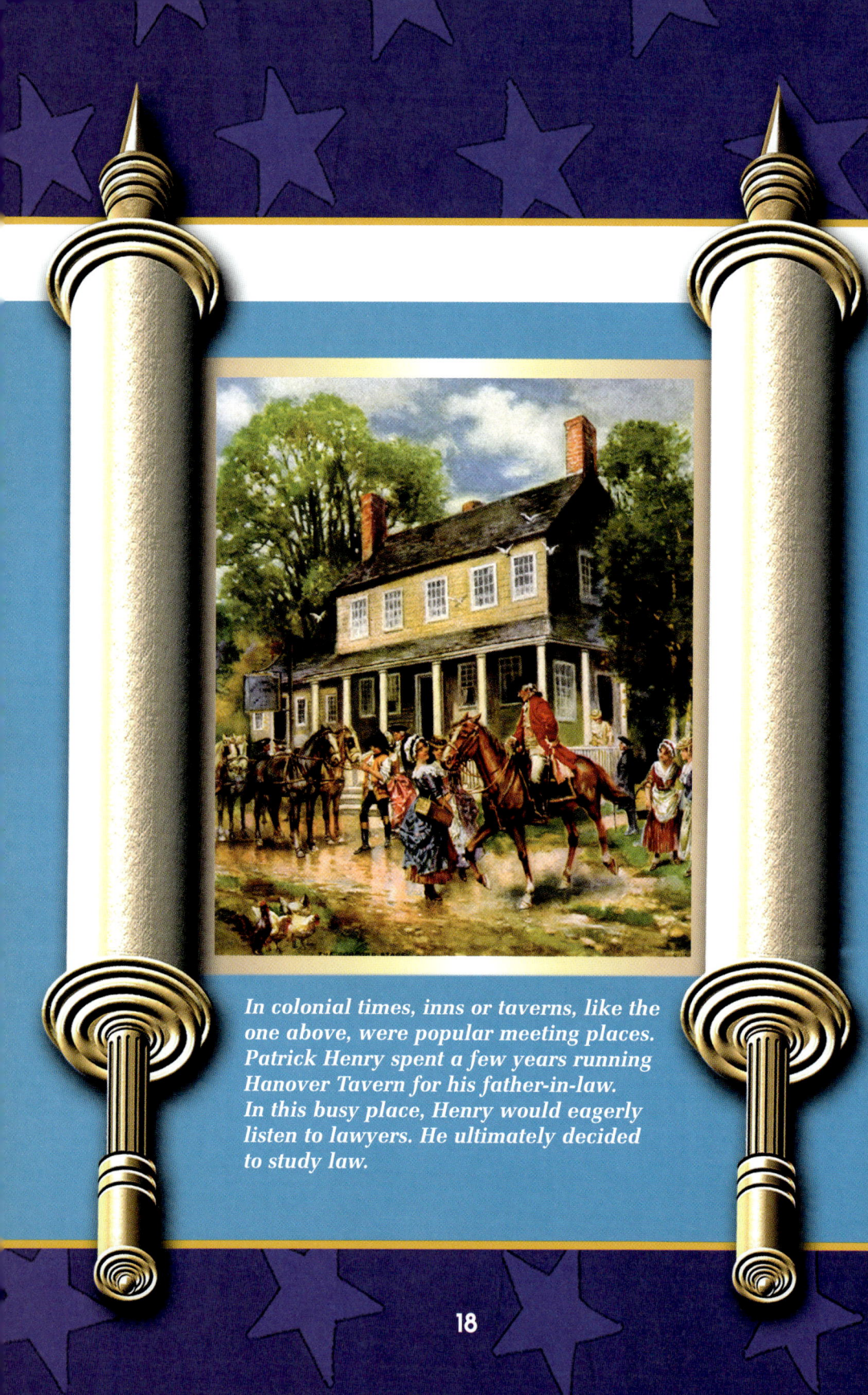

In colonial times, inns or taverns, like the one above, were popular meeting places. Patrick Henry spent a few years running Hanover Tavern for his father-in-law. In this busy place, Henry would eagerly listen to lawyers. He ultimately decided to study law.

CHAPTER 3

On His Way

Hanover Tavern was a busy social spot, and Henry was a good innkeeper. He took over the day-to-day business. He waited on customers, and he played the violin to entertain them.

More importantly, for Henry's sake anyway, he listened to the lawyers and judges who worked at the Hanover Courthouse. They often stopped at the tavern and discussed their cases. Henry spent much of his free time observing court. What he saw and heard inspired him. He couldn't farm, and he failed, not once, but twice, at running a store. The one thing he could do was talk. With his gift for gab, he often swayed listeners to his side of an argument. Becoming a lawyer seemed like the natural thing to do.

Unfortunately, there were no law schools in the colonies. Wealthy families sent their sons to London to study law. Those who couldn't afford a formal school apprenticed themselves to lawyers already in the colonies. Henry had a family and had to work. He couldn't run off to London; nor would he apprentice himself to anyone. There was only one solution—Patrick Henry would study law on his own, in secret.

Less than a year after moving into Hanover Tavern, and after only three months of study,[1] Henry made the trip to Williamsburg, the capital of Virginia, to get his law license. To pass the test, he

CHAPTER 3

impressed four of the county's most important lawyers, who quizzed him on all matters of the law. In April of 1760, Henry returned to Hanover Tavern a lawyer.

In the beginning, Henry took mostly small civil cases. He made a little money and even had time to hunt and fish. After all his disappointments, he was excited about his future.

In December 1763, Henry argued his first important case, the Parsons' Cause. He couldn't have known at the time how a conflict over tobacco would change his life.

Tobacco was so important that people paid their bills with it. For years, the price of tobacco remained steady at about two pence, or two pennies, a pound. Then, bad weather damaged the crops. Prices for the smaller harvest rose sharply.

Everyone who used tobacco to pay bills worried. Those who made obligations at the two-pence rate stood to lose a lot of money. For instance, suppose a planter agreed in January to pay a two-pence grocery bill with a pound of tobacco after the fall harvest. Then, because of the bad harvest, a pound of tobacco was suddenly worth six pence. Forced to pay that grocery bill with tobacco, the farmer lost four pence. The grocer then sold the tobacco and made four pence. But that wasn't the worst of it. The farmer had fewer pounds of tobacco to pay his debts. The farmers panicked.

Fortunately for the farmers, the House of Burgesses (an early form of legislature) responded. They passed a law that allowed farmers to pay bills in currency or tobacco. The farmer could sell his tobacco on the open market for six pence, then pay the grocer two pence in currency.

Everyone was satisfied with the law, except for the parsons. Back then, the counties paid their ministers of the Anglican Church from tax revenue. Each year, by law, these ministers received a salary of 16,000 pounds of tobacco. They saw the opportunity to raise their salaries and demanded tobacco instead of currency.

The Reverend Rowe, a divinity professor at the College of William and Mary, was particularly angry. He suggested the public should hang members of the House of Burgesses. He said that if any of them came to him for communion, he would turn them away.[2] The Reverend Rowe eventually apologized to avoid going to jail.

On His Way

The parsons turned to Governor Robert Dinwiddie, who hadn't yet signed the bill into law. He didn't like the bill, but he refused to veto it. The bill was popular with the common folk, and there were more common folk in Virginia than parsons.

The parsons then went to the King of England, who actually listened and vetoed the law. Fortunately for everyone, the tobacco crop of 1755 was better than expected and the Two-Penny Law was unneeded and forgotten—at least until 1758. That year, another poor tobacco crop created a second panic. To make matters worse, the king had raised taxes to pay for the French and Indian War.

The Burgesses enacted a second Two-Penny Law. This time they put the law into immediate practice. The king would take at least a year to veto it. By then, the crisis would be over. That year, the parsons collected a salary of 32,000 pence instead of 16,000 pounds of tobacco.

The king eventually vetoed the second law, and the parsons tried to collect back pay for 1758. The Reverend James Fontaine Maury of Hanover County filed suit on April 1, 1762. The suit named the county tax collectors as defendants. They chose an experienced lawyer, John Lewis, to represent them. The suit came to trial on November 3, 1763. Most people were disappointed when the parsons won.

Lewis had done the best he could and lost. He withdrew from the case and turned it over to Patrick Henry. All Henry had to do was represent the tax collectors to determine the award.

Henry had three weeks to prepare for what many saw as a hopeless cause. He asked no one for advice, relying on a pamphlet, "A Letter to the Clergy of Virginia," written by Richard Bland, an influential Burgess. This pamphlet urged the clergy to stop their protests because the safety of the people is the supreme law.[3]

Henry met a huge crowd in town on the morning of December 1, 1763. Almost everyone had a stake in the settlement. Henry knew that if the court awarded Maury a large amount, the county would raise taxes to pay it.

Henry saw his uncle and namesake, the Reverend Patrick Henry, approach the courthouse. Henry asked his uncle not to attend the session because he planned to speak harshly about the

CHAPTER 3

clergy and didn't want to upset his uncle. His uncle agreed and left.[4] Henry had a plan.

As the session got under way, Henry submitted a 1758 signed receipt for 144 pounds sterling and sat down. Peter Lyons, Maury's lawyer, then praised the Anglican Church in a long, dramatic speech.

Henry's opening remarks were awkward. Perhaps he was nervous because his father presided as judge. Henry could see the worried faces as he looked around the courtroom. Then, something came over him. He stood up straight, lowered his voice, and spoke with authority. He attacked the king, and turned the trial around.

"A king, by disallowing acts of this salutary nature, from being the father of his people, degenerated into a tyrant and forfeits all right to his subjects' obedience."[5] In other words, the king hadn't acted on his subjects' behalf when he struck down the Two-Penny Laws. The people needed the laws to protect their income.

Peter Lyons, the opposing lawyer, jumped to his feet and shouted, "The gentleman has spoken treason."[6]

Henry continued, and this time he attacked the clergy.

"Instead of feeding the hungry and clothing the naked, these rapacious harpies would, were their powers equal to their will, snatch from the hearth of their honest parishioner his last hoecake, from the widow and her orphan children their last milch [milk] cow, and the last bed—nay, the last blanket—from the lying-in woman."[7]

The courtroom erupted in anger. The clergymen in the audience jumped to their feet, knocking over their chairs and shouting as they hurried from the room. When the room settled down again, Henry urged the jury to punish Mr. Maury for daring to challenge the Two-Penny Laws. He also reminded the jury that they didn't have to award Mr. Maury a thing. He criticized the clergy and praised the law for another hour.[8] The jury took just five minutes to award Maury just one farthing.

The crowd erupted into loud cheers and rushed toward Henry. Still cheering and shouting, the triumphant crowd carried him out of the courtroom and into the courtyard on their shoulders. Patrick Henry had certainly found his niche.

Hanover County Court Days

A young girl finds out what it's like to be put on display in stocks

Colonial times could be boring, but not on Court Days. The first Thursday of every month, Hanover Courthouse filled with laughter, music, and great smells. That's because Hanover County's court was in session. (In addition to the monthly sessions, Hanover Court held a special quarterly session each March, June, September, and December.)

Hanover County Court Days were festive. People bet on horse races, and traveling groups performed all day. Peddlers in wagons and on foot set up camp and sold or traded their goods. A person didn't need business in court to come to town on Court Day. With few other forms of entertainment, angry lawyers and guilty criminals were fun to watch. Even children got a short reprieve from their chores. They spent the day playing and in general mischief. Boys wrestled and raced one another throughout the village. Girls giggled over apple peelings, using the shape of the fallen peel to divine the first letter of their future husband's name. Not all the day's business was court related. People paid outstanding bills and made deliveries. It wasn't unusual to find slaves, in chains, for sale at auction. People sentenced to the pillory or stocks were most unlucky, as huge crowds gathered to make fun of them. The lawyers, judges, and witnesses inside the courtroom shouted above the noise out in the courtyard to be heard.

Most people in the county came to court just for the fun of it—to visit friends and relatives and to enjoy the day. Hanover Tavern (where Patrick and Sarah Henry lived and worked for a while) would have been a busy place on court days. Besides feeding a large number of people, they probably would have rented most of the inn's beds to those too tired to travel home.

The French and Indian War started on American soil in 1754; it moved to Europe in 1756 and lasted seven more years. To pay for the war, Parliament passed a series of taxes on the colonists, including the Sugar Act and the Stamp Act.

CHAPTER 4

A Noble Patriot

Patrick Henry prospered over the next few years, and the colonists grew more frustrated with England. The Proclamation Line of 1763 closed the wilderness beyond the mountains to settlers; it also ordered those already living west of the mountains to return to the colonies.

Parliament also decided to tax the colonies to help pay for the French and Indian War. The colonists resented the tax because they hadn't approved of the war. England's head of the ministry (the term *prime minister* wasn't used then), Lord George Grenville, passed the Sugar Act in 1764. In truth, this act lowered the taxes on molasses. However, the colonists often bribed customs officials, so they rarely paid the tax. By lowering the tax, Grenville hoped to actually collect some of it.

Then Grenville suggested a stamp tax. While the colonists tolerated taxes (or duties) on imported goods, they flatly refused a tax on their livelihoods. The Stamp Act, which taxed all printed materials, affected almost everyone. It hit lawyers particularly hard. Every transaction was taxed—every license, official appointment, loan, bond, land survey, deed, warrant, diploma, bill of sale, and every other document required a stamp, purchased with cash. The stamp proved that the tax had been paid.

CHAPTER 4

Colonists were furious. While they fumed over the proposed stamp act in their homes and taverns, Henry practiced law. In 1764, he acquired a few thousand acres from his father and started to build a house. At about that time, his mentor, Thomas Johnson, encouraged him to run for the House of Burgesses, representing Louisa County. The Henrys didn't live in Louisa County, but that didn't matter. The law only required that representatives own property in the county that they represented. Henry ran unopposed, and on May 20, 1765, at the age of twenty-eight, he showed up for his first day in Virginia's House of Burgesses.

The Virginia House of Burgesses was the first representative government in the English colonies. The group included the county's governor, six councillors appointed by the governor, and seventeen elected members. They met in a small chamber and faced the Speaker, who wore a wig and gown.

Henry was younger than most of the other members. Certainly, he was less experienced in public service. Next to the other gentlemen in their silk coats, his shabby hunting clothes looked out of place.[1] Some members wore buckskins, but generally, even these men had thousands, often hundreds of thousands, of acres of land. In comparison, Henry's few thousand acres were insignificant, and most considered him to own nothing of value.

Members were equal by law. However, it didn't take Henry long to realize that a few wealthy men held the power. The governor's six councillors came from the most influential and wealthiest families in Virginia. Some of the more powerful members didn't like Henry because he was young and unsophisticated. He didn't respect their supremacy.

Being new, he could have sat quietly and let the more experienced members respond to the recently passed Stamp Act. Most Virginians considered the Stamp Act unlawful because only the legislators they elected could tax them. The Stamp Act came from Parliament, not their legislators. In the end, the experienced lawmakers did nothing. Many stayed home to tend to their farms. Henry then did what no one else seemed willing to do. He composed a list of five resolutions criticizing the Stamp Act.

A Noble Patriot

Emotions were high in 1765. Like many Americans, Patrick Henry was opposed to King George III's Stamp Act, which taxed the colonists for almost every transaction they made. In Virginia's House of Burgesses, Henry approached treason when he spoke of tyrants and their violent ends.

CHAPTER 4

On his twenty-ninth birthday, May 29, 1765, Henry presented his resolutions against the Stamp Act to the House of Burgesses. His resolutions spoke up for the colonies and demanded respect from Parliament. After only eight days as a member, he tipped the scales of power and led the charge of revolution.

After a heated debate, Henry defended his resolutions with a scandalous speech in which he referred to past tyrants that had met with execution or assassination.

"Caesar had his Brutus, Charles the First his Cromwell, and George the Third . . ."

Shouts of treason interrupted him. When the room was silent again, Henry finished.

". . . and George the Third may profit by their example. If this be treason, make the most of it."[2]

Once again, Henry triumphed. The house passed each of his five resolutions. (The Burgesses eventually rescinded the fifth resolution.) Newspapers published all five of them. Before long, all of the colonies followed Virginia's example.

The colonists simply refused to conduct court business or to pay the stamp tax. No one ever purchased a single stamp. After a while, the courts returned to normal. Courageous colonists did business without the stamps—in direct defiance of the law. In addition, the colonists called for a boycott against English goods, which proved to be far more damaging than their stamp revolt. In 1765, British sales in the colonies dropped by 13 percent.[3] Eventually, Parliament repealed the Stamp Act.

The relationship between the colonies and England remained tense, but business went on as usual for a few more years. Henry moved his family to a new home on Roundabout Creek in 1766. The courthouse was just six miles from his home, and Henry walked the distance so that he could hunt on the way. He often showed up in court wearing his hunting jacket. He was making a good living. He paid off most of his father's debts and loaned money to his father-in-law.

Another crisis that had been brewing was the Tea Act of 1773. This law allowed the British East India Company to sell tea in the colonies without paying an import tax. In contrast, all the colonial merchants paid an import tax by law. Given this special consideration, the company could charge less than the colonial merchants who paid the tax. The merchants had to pass the cost of the tax along to their customers.

The act gave the British East India Company an unfair advantage over the local merchants, who would eventually go out of business. If that happened, the company would gain a monopoly in tea imports. Then they could charge whatever they liked for their tea because there would be no one else selling it. Patriots called for a boycott on English tea, and the Henry family participated in it. England misjudged the colonists' desire for English tea. The colonists sipped homegrown brews and herbal teas instead.

When the *Dartmouth,* a British tea ship, arrived in Boston Harbor at the end of 1773, colonists protested. The ship sat in the harbor unable to unload for nearly three weeks—tensions in Boston were too high to risk a confrontation.

Under the law, the ship had twenty days to disburse its cargo. Otherwise, authorities could seize the ship's contents for nonpayment of import duties. If that happened, the tea would eventually make its way into stores. The colonists needed to avoid that possibility.

Finally, tensions rose to the point of vandalism. On December 16, 1773, Patriots disguised themselves as Native Americans and ran through the Boston streets to the harbor. There, they boarded the *Dartmouth* and her companion ships and tossed all the tea into the harbor—a total of 342 chests. The tea was worth a small fortune (well over half a million dollars by today's standards).

Boston's Tea Party caught on and New York held one. Maryland's Patriots liked the idea so much that they set fire to a tea ship. In the aftermath, Parliament enacted the Coercive Acts (known as the Intolerable Acts in the colonies) to punish Massachusetts. Until Boston paid for the tea, authorities allowed only military supplies, food, and fuel into the harbor. Demonstrators went to jail. British regiments marched into Boston to secure the town.

CHAPTER 4

> Bostonians protested the Tea Act of 1773 by dumping 342 chests of tea into the cold waters of Boston Harbor. New York and Maryland followed, hosting their own tea parties.

Virginia's House of Burgesses responded to the troops by calling for a day of prayer, to "turn the hearts of the King and Parliament to moderation and justice."[4] In response, an angry governor, Lord Dunmore, dissolved the Virginia House of Burgesses. Despite the governor's wrath, the day of prayer went on as planned and was a huge success. Colonists all over were outraged at the way England was treating Boston.

Governor Dunmore tried to warn the English. He reported that the colonies were supporting one another, spreading the flame of disobedience throughout the continent.

Patrick Henry's resolutions against the Stamp Act had been the sparks to light that flame.

Patrick Henry's Resolutions to the Stamp Act

On May 29, 1765, Patrick Henry, dressed in hunting clothes, presented five resolutions in response to Parliament's Stamp Act. Many of the Burgesses weren't at the session that day, claiming they needed to return home to tend to their farms. Most likely, they hoped to avoid exactly what happened—a fierce debate of the Stamp Act. Most of them didn't like the Stamp Act, but it was the law. To oppose it was dangerous. The following notes became Patrick Henry's five resolutions against the Stamp Act:

A stamp from the Stamp Act

> Resolved, That the settlers brought with them to this colony all the privileges, franchise, and immunities held by the people of Great Britain.
> Resolved, That the colonists are entitled to all the privileges, liberties, and immunities of citizens and natural born subjects as if they had been born within the realm of England.
> Resolved, That taxation of the people by themselves, or by persons chosen by themselves to represent them, is the distinguishing characteristic of British freedom.
> Resolved, That colonists should be governed by their own Assembly in the article of their taxes and internal police.
> Resolved, therefore, That the general assembly of the colony has the sole right and power to lay taxes and impositions upon the inhabitants of this colony. Every attempt to vest such power in any other persons would destroy both British and American freedom.[5]

All five resolutions passed that day. The fifth resolution passed by a simple majority of only one vote. However, the house eventually rescinded the fifth resolution because some of the Burgesses found it so provocative. Frankly, most of the Burgesses were afraid to push the king too far.

Using words, Patrick Henry rallied the American colonists to win their independence from Britain. As the governor of Virginia, he supported the war effort and American soldiers. After the war, Henry continued to serve the new government as a representative in the legislature.

CHAPTER 5

Forging a Nation

The colonies and England were close to war. England intended to tax the colonies without representation. It demanded that the colonists house British military officers—in their own homes! Officers chose space in any private home they liked. (This quartering provision was part of the Coercive Acts.)

A small group of Virginia's expelled Burgesses, including Patrick Henry, called for a Convention of the People. They declared the colony's authority and called on the other colonies to do so too. England should have listened to Lord Dunmore.

The Virginians still opposed one another on the opening day of the convention. Some still believed that the boycott would eventually work. In contrast, Henry felt the only course would be a display of strength and unity. Finally, the two sides agreed to a compromise: Beginning November 1, 1774, Virginia banned the import and purchase of slaves and all other British goods except medicines until the "redress of all such American grievances as may be defined at . . . the General Congress."[1] There it was—an official call for a unified convention of the colonies.

The group chose Henry and six other delegates to attend the First Continental Congress in Philadelphia. (The United States didn't exist yet, so they used the term *continental*.) Of the seven

CHAPTER 5

delegates, three opposed revolution, and three, including Henry, supported it. Only George Washington kept his feelings to himself. Virginians seemed equally divided.

The delegates met that first morning at New Tavern in Philadelphia. They cheered loudly. Then they walked through the streets of Philadelphia to Carpenters' Hall. Inside, they shouted and applauded. One can only imagine the excitement and fear these men must have felt during their march to destiny. They would build a new nation or hang for treason.

Coming together was an important but difficult step for the colonies to take. Many delegates in Philadelphia were reluctant to speak openly. To encourage independence was sedition, if not outright treason. To further hamper discussion, they were jealous

Patrick Henry traveled on horseback with two other Virginia delegates, George Washington and Edmund Pendleton, to the First Continental Congress in 1774. The other four delegates from Virginia were Richard Bland, Benjamin Harrison V, Richard Henry Lee, and Peyton Randolph.

Forging a Nation

of one another and simply couldn't act together as a group. They deliberated as Virginians, as New Yorkers, as Pennsylvanians, and so on. They could not see themselves as one group—Americans. Making toasts together was one thing; getting each delegate to stop thinking of himself as representing his own little country was going to be much harder. Henry rose to speak and reminded them that the British occupied Boston—and that was an attack against them all.

"The distinctions between Virginians, Pennsylvanians, New Yorkers, and New Englanders are no more. I am not a Virginian, but an American,"[2] he said.

From September 5 to October 12 of 1774, the delegates argued. Some still believed that a boycott would eventually force England to listen to their complaints. Henry no longer believed this was possible. The boycott might help the colonists come together and act as a group, but it was too little, too late. Henry knew that Congress must prepare for war.

In the end, the congress voted to continue the boycott and recommended that local committees enforce it. They also drew up a "bill of rights," which they sent to the king. Congress rejected Henry's first draft. John Adams and Richard Henry Lee prepared a new version, which Congress accepted and signed on October 20. Neither Patrick Henry nor John Adams expected the petition to the king to be successful. They were right. The king refused to read it.

After the convention, Patrick Henry returned home to Scotchtown Plantation in Hanover County. Sarah was terribly sick, and their children were worried and scared. Sarah suffered from depression. She had been unpredictable and unhappy since the birth of her last child, Edward, in early 1771. Her family irritated her, and she was prone to violent outbursts that endangered her children. Eventually, Patrick Henry refurbished the cellar and kept her in seclusion, far away from her children. The alternative was a mental asylum, and Patrick couldn't bear that for Sarah.

Her new lodgings were comfortable, and they suited her station. A beloved slave and their oldest daughter, Martha (Patsy), cared for her most of the time. When Patrick was home, he sat with her and even fed her.

CHAPTER 5

Unable to help Sarah beyond keeping her safe, Patrick threw himself into the Patriots' cause at home. He met with gentlemen from all over the county. He used his famous persuasive talents to convince his friends and neighbors that England planned to use force against them.

Maryland and Virginia organized militias, and Henry prepared for the Second Virginia Convention.

For Henry, the convention probably came much too quickly. Sarah died in early February, and he sorely grieved for her. Yet, for just a few days, he put his grief aside and traveled to Richmond.

On March 21, 1775, he met old friends and adversaries. They spent two days debating. Some delegates still believed that a boycott would have the desired effect. An outright revolution would be going too far. Henry's mind was set. He had come with one purpose—to convince Virginians to prepare to defend themselves against British forces. He was convinced that Britain would—sooner rather than later—use British troops against them.

"If we wish to be free, we must fight!—I repeat it, sir, we must fight!"[3] he insisted.

"Shall we gather strength by irresolution and inaction?" he asked. "Shall we acquire the effective means of resistance . . . by hugging the delusive phantom of Hope until our enemies shall have bound us hand and foot?"[4]

Henry knew that the colonists no longer had a choice. The point of no return had come and gone. Patrick Henry wanted freedom, and he was willing to die for it.

Henry's famous "give me liberty, or give me death" speech took its place in history and became one of the most famous calls to war. The inspired delegates gave Henry the militia he wanted and made him the chairman of its planning committee. Before closing, the delegates chose Henry and six others to attend the next Continental Congress. He was an inspirational sight as he traveled home on horseback. He carried a banner that read "Liberty or Death" through every county until he reached home.

A few weeks later, on April 20, Governor Dunmore's men, under the cover of darkness, raided Williamsburg's public magazine. The outraged citizens gathered at the governor's mansion

Forging a Nation

the next morning. That gunpowder belonged to the citizens of Williamsburg, not the British! Dunmore tried to lie his way out of a riot by telling them that he had protected them from a slave uprising. Virginians knew he was lying, but he avoided an outright riot.

Henry demanded that the governor pay for or return their gunpowder. To show the governor just how serious he was, Henry and a group of about 150 men left for Williamsburg on May 2. By the time they reached the outskirts of the city, the group had grown to 5,000. Henry and the governor's officials exchanged many tense messages, and finally the British paid for the gunpowder.

Henry returned to Hanover County, where he was hailed a hero. Meanwhile, Governor Dunmore officially spoke against him. He warned that anyone who helped Henry in any way would offend the king. Then, he deserted the governor's mansion and took his family to live aboard a British military ship in the harbor.

Henry traveled straight to the Second Continental Congress in Philadelphia. Held May to December of 1775, the Congress created a Continental Army and appointed George Washington as its commander. This army was the first official American army. The action came none too soon. In June, with the Congress still convened, Massachusetts militiamen fought the British at Bunker Hill—twice. The Continental Congress also urged each of the colonies to write and adopt its own state constitution.

In his absence, Virginia delegates appointed Patrick Henry Colonel of the First Virginia Regiment, even though he had no formal military training or experience. Henry left Philadelphia for Richmond to take his command.

Despite his position as commander, he stayed behind to protect Williamsburg while a more experienced soldier, Colonel William Woodford, led Virginia's rebel forces into the first southern land battle. The Battle of Great Bridge lasted only thirty minutes, but it put the English on notice—the southern rebels could and would fight!

Henry was glad for the victory, but he was also disappointed at being left behind. In February of 1776, he faced the unhappy truth—he was a great speaker, but he was not a soldier any more than he was a farmer or a storekeeper. In fact, many experienced

CHAPTER 5

In June 1775, while Henry and other delegates to the Second Continental Congress met in Philadelphia, militiamen fought the British at Bunker Hill near Boston, Massachusetts. The British won this first major battle of the war, even though they lost more soldiers and officers than the Patriots did.

military men openly opposed his appointment. Henry resigned his military post.

For better or worse, Henry didn't have much time to feel sorry for himself. He and his half brother, John Syme, once again, were called to represent Hanover County. Delegates to Virginia's Fifth Revolutionary Convention wrote and adopted a new state constitution that summer. The convention closed on June 29, 1776. In their final act, they elected Henry as the first governor of the independent commonwealth of Virginia.

Forging a Nation

Virginians weren't the only ones busy drafting important and history-making documents. Thomas Jefferson was in Philadelphia writing the Declaration of Independence. On July 4, 1776, Congress adopted the Declaration of Independence. John Hancock, President of the Continental Congress, sent copies to the New Jersey and Delaware legislatures. The *Pennsylvania Evening Post* printed the entire text on July 6. Interestingly, Patrick Henry did not sign the Declaration of Independence.

On October 9, as the revolution swung into full motion, Governor Henry married Dorothea Dandridge. "Dolly" was the granddaughter of a previous Virginia governor, Alexander Spotswood. She was much younger than Patrick, and over the next twenty years, she presented him with eleven more children.

As governor, Patrick Henry did all he could to help General George Washington and the Continental Army. He insisted that Congress inoculate the men for smallpox, and pay for it. When Washington's army was freezing at Valley Forge, Pennsylvania, Governor Henry sent 10,000 pounds of meat, 2,000 bushels of salt, blankets, and other supplies. He sent lead and sulfur to the troops for bullets and gunpowder. Without the governor's quick response to the army's needs, the army might have had to disband.[5]

Governor Henry believed that Kentucky settlers were in danger, so Virginia declared Kentucky a county of Virginia. That entitled Kentucky to Virginia's protection. George Rogers Clark met with Governor Henry to devise a plan for driving the British out of the western portions of Virginia. Clark was successful. The lands he seized from the British became the states of Ohio, Indiana, Illinois, Michigan, Wisconsin, and half of Minnesota.[6]

Henry served three one-year terms as governor of Virginia. He retired in 1779 to Leatherwood, a huge plantation near the North Carolina border in Henry County (named for him). He and his family lived there quietly during the last years of the war.

The citizens of Henry County elected Patrick Henry to every assembly from 1780 on, but his health often kept him from attending. The new legislature looked very different from the House of Burgesses. Most members owned small farms and only a few

CHAPTER 5

slaves. They were tobacco farmers and hunters, and they debated and made laws wearing buckskin jackets and boots. There were no wigs and few silks, and the atmosphere was more relaxed.

Finally, in the spring of 1782, Patrick Henry and his family rejoiced when they received the news of Cornwallis' October surrender at Yorktown.

In 1784, Patrick and Dorothea Henry, returned to Richmond when Virginia elected Patrick governor for a fourth term. (He was reelected again the next year.) Richmond too had changed. Less than ten years had passed since he'd visited the small village and made his famous speech that inspired the Burgesses to war. In 1784, Richmond had a population of 15,000.

Despite his fame, he never took himself too seriously. Even while living in the governor's mansion, he took care of his own fire and was often seen out riding a horse with his children—one in front and one in back. In 1786, he left office. He had a house full of children to raise and provide for. (Patrick Henry had seventeen children with two wives.) He wanted to educate his boys and provide dowries for his girls.

About this time, the Philadelphia Convention convened in secret. Many members of the new government weren't satisfied with the country's Articles of Confederation. The Articles of Confederation was a plan drawn up by the First Continental Congress to help the new states cooperate with one another.

The Federalists wanted a strong central government with authority over the states. The new governor of Virginia, Edmund Randolph, tried to appoint Henry to represent Virginia, but Henry refused to go. He was strongly opposed to a central government. That made him an anti-Federalist and as such, he supported powerful states. He preferred the current Articles of Confederation because it required all states to unanimously approve any amendment. In the end, the convention produced our Constitution, which supports a strong central government.

George Washington sent Patrick Henry a copy of the new Constitution. His reply was polite, considering how betrayed he must have felt: "I have to lament that I cannot bring my mind to accord with the proposed Constitution."[7]

At a special convention beginning June 2, 1788, Henry argued against the Constitution. For days he argued against a powerful central government, far removed from the citizens of Virginia, that "will plunge us into misery, and our republic will be lost."[8]

The words *We, the people* angered him. He declared it should be "We, the states."[9]

Eventually, he realized that he could not overturn the Constitution. He concentrated on a bill of rights that would protect the rights of individual citizens. He also wanted amendments to protect state and local governments. The convention ratified the Constitution, but only after Henry convinced them to add ten amendments. Those amendments became our Bill of Rights, which Congress adopted in December of 1791.

Soon, Dorothea and Patrick Henry retired—again. At Red Hill, one of Henry's three plantations, he played with his children and grandchildren while he watched a young United States grow.

The new government wasn't about to let go of Patrick Henry if they could help it. Virginia's governor Henry "Light Horse Harry" Lee tried to appoint Patrick Henry to a vacant seat in the new U.S. Senate. President Washington tried to make him Chief Justice of the Supreme Court, Secretary of State, and Vice President of the United States. Henry said no to all of these appointments. Finally, President Washington convinced him to return to Virginia's legislature in 1799. He won the election, but as fate would have it, he didn't serve. Patrick Henry died on June 6, 1799, just a few months after the election.

Looking back, it's easy to see that all the founding fathers played a huge role in our nation's quest for independence. However, Patrick Henry, above all the others, stirred something in the American people. He inspired colonists to be more than British subjects. His words cut through individual and petty fears and inspired a disconnected assemblage to create a truly great nation—the United States of America.

America's Bill of Rights

Patrick Henry demanded that the Constitution protect the rights of individual citizens. Without his fierce insistence, it's possible we wouldn't have the first ten amendments, which we call the Bill of Rights. These amendments follow:

Amendment I. Congress shall make no law respecting an establishment of religion, or prohibiting the free exercise thereof; or abridging the freedom of speech, or of the press . . .

Amendment II. A well regulated Militia, being necessary to the security of a free State, the right of the people to keep and bear Arms, shall not be infringed.

Amendment III. No Soldier shall, in time of peace be quartered in any house, without the consent of the Owner . . .

Amendment IV. The right of the people to be secure in their persons, houses, papers, and effects, against unreasonable searches and seizures, shall not be violated . . .

Amendment V. No person shall be held to answer for a capital, or otherwise infamous crime, unless on a presentment or indictment of a Grand Jury . . .

Amendment VI. In all criminal prosecutions, the accused shall enjoy the right to a speedy and public trial, by an impartial jury of the State and district wherein the crime shall have been committed . . .

Amendment VII. In Suits at common law, where the value in controversy shall exceed twenty dollars, the right of trial by jury shall be preserved . . .

Amendment VIII. Excessive bail shall not be required, nor excessive fines imposed, nor cruel and unusual punishments inflicted.

Amendment IX. The enumeration in the Constitution, of certain rights, shall not be construed to deny or disparage others retained by the people.

Amendment X. The powers not delegated to the United States by the Constitution, nor prohibited by it to the States, are reserved to the States, respectively, or to the people.

Chapter Notes

Chapter One: The Voice of Revolution
1. William Safire, *Lend Me Your Ears: Great Speeches in History* (New York: W. W. Norton & Company, 1992), p. 87.
2. Ibid., p. 89.

Chapter Two: Far From the Watchful Eye of England
1. George F. Willison, *Patrick Henry and His World* (Garden City, New York: Doubleday and Company, Inc., 1969), p. 24.
2. Ibid., p. 25.
3. Steven W. Allen, *Founding Fathers: Uncommon Heroes* (Mesa, Arizona: Legal Awareness Series, Inc., 2003), p. 118.
4. Willison, p. 27.
5. Henry Mayer, *A Son of Thunder* (New York: Franklin Watts, 1986), p. 168.
6. Ibid., p. 169.
7. Ibid.

Chapter Three: On His Way
1. Steven W. Allen, *Founding Fathers: Uncommon Heroes* (Mesa, Arizona: Legal Awareness Series, Inc., 2003), p. 120.
2. George F. Willison, *Patrick Henry and His World* (Garden City, New York: Doubleday and Company, Inc., 1969), pp. 70–71.
3. Ibid., pp. 74–75.
4. Ibid., p. 76.
5. Ibid., pp. 79–80.
6. Ibid., p. 80.
7. Ibid., pp. 80–81.
8. Allen, p. 123.

Chapter Four: A Noble Patriot
1. Steven W. Allen, *Founding Fathers: Uncommon Heroes* (Mesa, Arizona: Legal Awareness Series, Inc., 2003), p. 124.
2. Ibid., p. 125.
3. Daniel J. Boorstin, and Brooks Mather Kelley, with Ruth Frankel Boorstin, *A History of the United States* (Upper Saddle River, New Jersey: Pearson Prentice Hall, 2005), p. 79.
4. George F. Willison, *Patrick Henry and His World* (Garden City, New York: Doubleday and Company, Inc., 1969), p. 223.
5. Allen, pp. 124–125.

Chapter Five: Forging a Nation
1. Henry Mayer, *A Son of Thunder* (New York: Franklin Watts, 1986), p. 202.
2. Ibid., pp. 212–213.
3. Ibid., p. 244.
4. Ibid., p. 245.
5. Steven W. Allen, *Founding Fathers: Uncommon Heroes* (Mesa, Arizona: Legal Awareness Series, Inc., 2003), p. 134.
6. Ibid., p. 134.
7. Mayer, p. 376.
8. The Constitution Society, "Virginia Ratifying Convention, June 4, 1788," http://www.constitution.org/rc/rat_va_03.htm
9. Ibid.

Chronology

1736	Patrick Henry is born on May 29 in Hanover County, Virginia.
1748	The Henrys move to Mount Brilliant.
1751	Patrick Henry apprentices to a storekeeper.
1752	He sets up storekeeping with his brother William, but the store fails.
1754	He marries Sarah Shelton; they move to Piney Slash.
1757	Fire destroys the Henry home at Piney Slash. Patrick Henry opens a second store, but it fails.
1759	The Henrys move to Hanover Tavern.
1760	Patrick Henry is admitted to the bar.
1763	Patrick Henry criticizes king and clergy in the Parsons' Cause case.
1765	He is elected to the Virginia House of Burgesses and introduces resolutions against the Stamp Act.
1774	He is elected to and attends the First Continental Congress in Philadelphia.
1775	Sarah Henry dies. Patrick Henry is elected to and attends the Second Virginia Convention in March, where he gives his most famous speech, "Give me liberty or give me death." He marches on Williamsburg to demand Governor Dunmore return public gunpowder on May 2. He attends the Second Continental Congress. He is elected Colonel of the First Virginia Regiment and commander in chief of the Virginia militia on August 26.
1776	He resigns his military appointment on February 28. He is elected to attend Virginia's Fifth Revolutionary Convention and is elected the first governor of the independent commonwealth of Virginia. He marries Dorothea Dandridge.
1779	Patrick Henry moves to Henry County. The citizens of Henry County elect him to the General Assembly.
1784	He is elected to a fourth term as governor of Virginia.
1785	He is elected to a fifth term as governor of Virginia.
1787	He declines to serve at the Constitutional Convention in Philadelphia.
1788	He is elected to the Virginia House of Delegates and to the Virginia Convention.
1799	Patrick Henry dies on June 6, at age sixty-three.

Timeline in History

1607	Jamestown is founded in Virginia.
1631–1733	Proprietary colonies of Maryland, Carolina, New Jersey, Pennsylvania, Delaware, and Georgia are founded.
1675	Charles II creates the Lords of Trade in London to manage colonial affairs.
1696	Navigation Laws mandate all trade between colonies and England must be transported in English-built ships.
1699	The General Assembly moves Virginia's capitol to Williamsburg.
1735	The trial of John Peter Zenger establishes freedom of the press.
1754	The French and Indian War begins on American soil.
1763	The French and Indian War ends. The Proclamation Line of 1763 uses the mountains as a natural boundary between settlers and Native Americans.
1764	Parliament passes the Sugar Act.
1765	Parliament passes the Stamp Act.
1766	Parliament repeals the Stamp Act; it passes the Declaratory Act, which states that Parliament has the power to make all laws for Americans.
1767	The Townshend Acts reorganize the customs service and imposes new taxes on imports.
1770	Parliament repeals most of the Townshend Acts, but keeps the tax on tea.
1773	Boston Patriots organize the Boston Tea Party.
1774	The Coercive Acts, known as the Intolerable Acts in the colonies, are enacted. First Continental Congress convenes in Philadelphia.
1775	The Revolutionary War begins. The Second Continental Congress is held in Philadelphia.
1776	The Declaration of Independence is adopted.
1777	Washington's troops suffer through the winter at Valley Forge.
1781	Articles of Confederation are adopted. Cornwallis surrenders at Yorktown, ending the war.
1783	Treaty of Paris is signed. British troops leave New York. George Washington resigns as commander.
1789	The U.S. Constitution is ratified. The French Revolution begins. George Washington becomes the first President of the United States.
1803	The United States buys Louisiana from the French.
1812	The War of 1812; the British burn the White House in Washington, D.C.
1820	Congress passes the Missouri Compromise.
1838	Army relocates 15,000 Native Americans from the east to Oklahoma territory in what becomes known as the Trail of Tears.
1844	Samuel Morse sends the first telegraph message from Baltimore to Washington.
1847	The Post Office Department issues the first national postage stamps.
1848	Workers at Sutter's Mill in California discover gold.
1852	Harriet Beecher Stowe publishes *Uncle Tom's Cabin,* an antislavery book.

Further Reading

For Young Adults
Dupuy, Colonel R. Ernest, and Colonel Trevor N. Dupuy. *An Outline History of the American Revolution.* New York: Harper & Row, Publishers, 1975.
Editors of Time-Life Books. *The American Story: The Revolutionaries.* Alexandria, Virginia: Time-Life Books, 1996.
Hakim, Joy. *From Colonies to Country.* New York: Oxford University Press, 1999.
Kukla, Amy, and Jon Kukla. *Patrick Henry: Voice of the Revolution.* New York: The Rosen Publishing Group, Inc., 2002.
Langguth, A. J. *Patriots: The Men Who Started the American Revolution.* New York: Simon and Schuster, 1988.
Rinaldi, Ann. *Or Give Me Death.* San Diego: Gulliver Books, Harcourt, Inc., 2003.

Works Consulted
Allen, Steven W. *Founding Fathers: Uncommon Heroes.* Mesa, Arizona: Legal Awareness Series, Inc., 2003.
Boorstin, Daniel J., and Brooks Mather Kelley, with Ruth Frankel Boorstin. *A History of the United States.* Upper Saddle River, New Jersey: Pearson Prentice Hall, 2005.
Complete text of Patrick Henry's "Give me liberty or give me death" speech given on March 23, 1775, at the Second Virginia Convention
http://www.americanrhetoric.com/speeches/patrickhenrygivemeliberty.html
Complete text of The Tea Act
http://ahp.gatech.edu/tea_act_bp_1773.html
The Constitution Society, "Virginia Ratifying Convention, June 4, 1788," http://www.con-stitution.org/rc/rat_va_03.htm
Mayer, Henry. *A Son of Thunder: Patrick Henry and the American Republic.* New York: Franklin Watts, 1986.
Safire, William. *Lend Me Your Ears: Great Speeches in History.* New York: W. W. Norton & Company, 1992.
Willison, George F. *Patrick Henry and His World.* Garden City, New York: Doubleday and Company, Inc., 1969.

On the Internet
Time Line, America During the Age of Revolution, 1764–1775
http://memory.loc.gov/ammem/bdsds/timeline.html
The Bill of Rights
http://www.archives.gov/national_archives_experience/charters/bill_of_rights_tran-script.html
The Declaration of Independence
http://www.archives.gov/national_archives_experience/charters/declaration_tran-script.html
The Constitution
http://www.archives.gov/national_archives_experience/charters/constitution_tran-script.html
Revolutionary War Resources
http://www.ushistory.org/declaration/related/index.htm
Redhill: Patrick Henry National Memorial
http://www.redhill.org

Glossary

abolish (uh-BAH-lish)
To do away with.

back country
The unsettled areas of wilderness to the west of the Atlantic coastline in colonial America.

boycott (BOY-kot)
To refuse to buy or support a particular product or company.

degenerate (dee-JEH-neh-rayt)
To decline into an inferior state.

delegate (DEH-luh-git)
A representative to a conference or convention.

deliberate (duh-LIH-ber-ayt)
To consider thoughtfully; to discuss or debate with others.

farthing (FAR-thing)
A coin worth one quarter of a cent.

harpy (HAR-pee)
In mythology, a creature that was half woman, half bird; harpies stole food from a starving prophet.

hoe-cake
A small cake made of cornmeal.

hypocrisy (hih-PAH-krah-see)
To speak out against something while doing it yourself.

insidious (in-SIH-dee-us)
Something really bad; evil.

lenity (LEE-nuh-tee)
Clemency; going easy on a punishment.

magazine (MAA-guh-zeen)
A building for storing ammunition and gunpowder.

monopoly (muh-NAH-puh-lee)
A group that controls all the sales of a particular product.

parson (PAR-son)
A minister.

pillory (PIH-luh-ree)
A wooden frame on a post with holes for the head and hands in which those guilty of minor offenses were locked as punishment.

pound sterling
A unit of money worth 100 pence.

quartering (KWAR-ter-ing)
Putting soldiers up in private homes instead of a fort or barracks.

rapacious (ruh-PAY-shus)
Excessively selfish or greedy.

rescind (ree-SIND)
To cancel something that has already been approved.

salutary (SAH-lyoo-tay-ree)
Beneficial; intending to correct a faulty ruling.

sedition (seh-DIH-shen)
Organized rebellion against the law.

stock
A wooden frame on a post with holes for the ankles and sometimes the wrists in which those guilty of minor offenses were locked as punishment.

veto (VEE-toe)
To disapprove a bill that has been passed by the legislature.

Index

Adams, John 35
Articles of Confederation 40
Battle of Great Bridge, the 37
Bill of Rights 35, 41, 42
Boston 10, 27, 29, 35
Boston Tea Party 29-30
British East India Company 28-29
Bunker Hill 37, 38
Carpenters' Hall (Independence Hall) 34
Clark, George Rogers 39
Coercive Acts (Intolerable Acts) 29, 33
Constitution 37, 38, 40-41, 42
Continental Army 11, 37, 39
Continental Congress 11, 33-35, 37, 39, 40
Convention of the People 33
Declaration of Independence 39
Dinwiddie, Robert, Governor 21
Dunmore, Lord 30, 33, 36, 37
Federalists 40
First Continental Congress 33-35, 40
First Virginia Regiment 37
French and Indian War 16, 21, 24, 25
George III, King 7-8, 9, 10, 11, 14, 21, 22, 30, 31, 37
Grenville, Lord George 25
Hancock, John 39
Hanover County 13, 15, 21, 23, 35, 37, 38
Hanover Courthouse 16, 19, 21, 23, 28
Hanover Tavern 16, 19, 20, 23
Henry, Dorothea Dandridge (wife) 39, 40, 41
Henry, John (father) 13, 14, 15, 16
Henry, Martha (daughter) 35
Henry, Patrick
    birth of 13
    career of 15-16, 19-22, 26, 28, 33, 37, 39
    childhood of 13-16
    children of 16, 35, 39, 40, 41
    as Colonel 37-38
    death of 41
    education of 14, 19
    as governor of Virginia 38, 39, 40
    homes of 13, 16, 28, 35, 39, 41
    marriages of 16, 39
    parents of 13
    slavery, views on 17
    speeches of 6, 8-10, 28, 31, 34, 35, 36, 40
    religion of 14
Henry, Reverend Patrick (uncle) 21-22
Henry, Sarah Winston Syme (mother) 13, 14
Henry, William (brother) 15
Henry, Sarah Shelton (wife) 16, 23, 35-36
House of Burgesses 20, 21, 26, 27, 28, 30, 31, 33, 39, 40
Jefferson, Thomas 17, 39
Johnson, Thomas 26
Lee, Henry (Light Horse Harry) 41
Lee, Richard Henry 34, 35
Lewis, John 21
Louisa County 26
Loyalist(s) 7, 8, 11
Maury, James Fontaine Reverend 21-22
New Tavern 34
Patriot(s) 7, 11, 29, 36
Parsons' Cause 20-22
Philadelphia 33, 34, 37, 38, 40
Philadelphia Convention 40
Proclamation Line of 1763 25
Randolph, Edmund 40
Richmond 36, 37, 40
Rowe, Reverend 20
St. John's Church 7
Second Continental Congress 37, 38
Second Virginia Convention 6, 7, 36
Shelton, John (father-in-law) 16
Stamp Act 25-27, 28, 30, 31
Studley Farm 13, 14, 16
Sugar Act 25
Syme, John 13
Syme, John Jr. (half brother) 16, 38
Tea Act of 1773 28-29
tobacco 16, 20-21, 39
Two-Penny Law 21, 22
Valley Forge 39
Virginia, colony 6, 7, 14, 17, 21, 26, 28, 30, 33, 37
Virginia, commonwealth of 38-41
Virginia militia 13, 36
Virginia's Fifth Revolutionary Convention 38
Washington, George 11, 34, 37, 39, 40, 41
Williamsburg 19, 36, 37